Contents

Non-Piece Pages

Pieces

Introduction

Note from the Composer/Author

Mis-Match was created with the sole purpose of being able to get a late-beginner/intermediate pianist to play music in different styles, from baroque, to minimalism, to jazz; this book has a large range of music for the piano.

In the modern world there are a lot of music books that are specific to a style, maybe you've found a book for classical music, blues music or maybe even music to practice a specific technique, but there aren't a lot of books out there that contain them all together. In this book you will find a range of pieces from all those styles and much, more!

Relax and enjoy playing some original pieces where there's guaranteed to be something for everyone.

About the pieces

The pieces have all got fingering written on them to help guide you on what fingers to use and when to use them. However, these are only a guide and you are more than welcome to change it if you feel you have a better way of playing it.

Words in bold (in the piece's descriptions) are words that can be found in the glossary at the back of this book, in case you don't know what they mean.

About the Author/Composer

Josh Rowe is a 17 year old composer from Wiltshire, England, who is currently studying music performance and technology at college and is going onto study a BA Honours in popular music at University. He has played the keyboard/piano since the age of 11 and the saxophone since the age of 12.

Practice Techniques

Don't know how to start practicing the piece? Struggling to play one or more of the pieces?... Don't Worry!!! Try these 5 things and you'll be playing the piece in no time.

1. Slow the piece down

- Try playing the piece at a slower tempo than it says to play. Start at maybe half tempo (e.g. if the tempo says 120 bpm try playing it at 60 bpm) and then adjust it from there.
- Once you have learned it at half tempo, start increasing the speed gradually by maybe 5-10 bpm at a time until you are able to play it at the full tempo.
- A study by Robert Duke of the University of Texas showed that this was the single best way to learn a piece in the most effective amount of time possible (so TRY IT !!!)

2. Play one hand at a time

- Start practicing the piece using only one hand. Try playing the right hand first, then the left hand; then once you've learned it separately, try bringing both hands together to play the whole piece.

3. Play one section of a piece at a time

- Rather than playing the entire piece at once, which might seem daunting, try playing the piece, one section at a time. That way if you find there's a part of the piece that you can't quite get right, you can focus on it until you can play it correctly.

4. Use a metronome

- By using a metronome, you can keep a strict beat going whilst you play along, to ensure you don't deviate from the original tempo. (Some pieces may not have a strict tempo, so be careful you don't use a metronome too much with these).
- You can use this alongside point No. 1, where you can set a tempo for you to play, and keep to that tempo.
- Don't worry if you don't have a metronome, there are loads of apps with metronome's that you can download for free.

5. Take a Break

- If you're still struggling to play a piece of music, or if you've been playing for a long time (over an hour), then have a break and try playing something else. You can always come back to it later on!

If You're Bored

Already learned the pieces? Don't know what to do next? Try these fun activities, which you can use on any of the pieces in this book!

Try playing the pieces at different speeds

- If you have already learned the pieces, have a go at playing them at different speeds than they are supposed to be. How quickly can you play the piece whilst keeping it accurate? How slowly can you play it whilst still keeping a beat going?
- Be careful not to hurt your fingers by trying to play them too quickly for too long!!!

Try working out the chords

- There are a lot of different chords used in this book. Have a go at seeing if you can work out what some of these are for yourself.
- Some chords are tricky to work out so if you can't by yourself, ask a musical friend to help or maybe even your music teacher if you have one.

Try improvising a melody

- Some pieces already have improvisation sections but if you still want more improv then try playing a piece with a different melody.

Try coming up with your own piece

- If just creating a melody is too easy then pick a piece from this book that you really like and see if you can come up with a piece of your own that sounds similar.
- Or if you don't want to choose a piece to base it off of, try to create a one from scratch.

Take a picture with the book and post it on social media

- If you've done everything, post a picture of the book on social media using the hashtag #mis-match so we can see how much you're enjoying it.

The Graceful Blues

- The piece's focus is on the use of the **12 bar blues**, which is shown by the notes in the left hand, so try to ensure that the notes in the bass clef are played strongly.
- There is an improvisation section in the middle that repeats round twice, which is common of blues style music. The notes written in brackets are the notes you should use. Try using them in different orders!
- There are some **Grace Notes (acciaccatura's)** littered throughout the main melody, try to ensure they are played quickly and try to add some into your improvisation later on.

Close Encounters of the Thirds Kind

- The piece's focus is on the use of **major and minor thirds**, so try to ensure these are played crisply.
- Watch out for the stabs at bar 13 and 17, try to ensure these are **staccato** and **sforzando.**
- At the end of the piece there is a **ritardando**, so try to slow the piece down at this point.

No Rest For the Wicked

- The focus of this piece are the rests, so try to ensure that you do not hold notes down where there should be a rest.
- There are a lot of repeats and jumps in this piece, so try to ensure you know where you are going, especially for the **D.S. (Dal Segno) al Coda** and **Coda.**
- Watch the **syncopation** at bar 16, as it is slightly different to anywhere else in the piece.

1.
2. D.S. al Coda
mf
mp

Summertime Swing

- The focus of this piece is on the left hand **staccato**. Try to keep each chord detached from the next to create the right feel for the piece. Try not to let the notes in the left hand become louder than the notes in the right hand!
- Try to ensure that the middle section is a lot quieter than the start and end sections but try to keep the beat going.

Over the Hills

- The focus of this piece is on playing the right hand **quavers** as accurately as possible, so try to ensure these are all the same length.
- The other part of this piece that you need to look out for is the left hand crossing over the right hand, so try to ensure you move your hand quickly enough to reach these notes in time.

Minimal Time

- The piece's focus is on the technique of **minimalism** and playing **rubato**, so watch out for little changes every few bars and try to make sure you play every note correctly.
- The **dynamics** change a lot. Try to remember to play each section at the right volume.
- There are **pauses (fermatas)** near the end of the piece. Try not to rush over these as they help to bring the piece to a slow and peaceful conclusion.

rit. (2nd time)
a tempo.
p
mf
f
sudden stop.
2nd time only
molto expressivo.
pp
ppp

15

On the Carousel

- The pieces focus is on crossing over the left hand, so try to ensure you bring your second finger over your thumb whenever this occurs throughout the piece.
- Try to ensure that the **middle 8** section has a softer **dynamic** than the rest of the piece.
- There are a lot of 'clashy' notes at the end of the piece, but the tune is still the same as the beginning. Try to play the tune louder than the other notes so that the 'clashy' notes don't stand out as much.

Out with the New, In with the Old

- The piece has a focus of playing in a **baroque** style, which means the left hand moves around a lot more than in other pieces. Try to focus on playing hands separately first to get the left hand correct.
- There are multiple **ritardando's** including one at the end, try to remember to slow down when you see it as this helps to end the piece.

18
mf
5
22
rit.
ad lib.
mp
f
1 3 5

Give me a Dance

- The piece's focus is playing in a fast **boogie woogie** style, the left hand being consistent ensures that this style is maintained throughout the piece so try to keep it the same throughout.
- There is an improvised solo in the middle, use the notes of the C major scale so have fun playing around with them.

To Coda

Improv Solo

D.S. al Coda

Haunted House

- The focus of this piece is on playing the **Alberti bass** in the left hand consistently. Try to keep your wrist and fingers relaxed so it is easier to play it.
- There is also a large number of **accidentals** in this piece so try to look ahead carefully so you don't miss any of them.

Glossary

12 Bar Blues: A chord progression that is 12 bars long and uses the 1st, 4th and 5th chords of any musical scale.

A-H

Accelerando (accel): Gradual increase in speed.

Accent: A stronger attack/force placed on a particular note.

Accidentals: Is a note that is not part of the scale shown by the key signature. It will usually have a sharp, flat or natural symbol next to it.

Ad Lib: Play the section of the music 'as you like'.

Alberti Bass: An accompaniment using broken chords with a specific order of notes used (lowest note of the chord, highest, middle, highest).

Baroque: A period of history between 1600 and 1740.

Boogie Woogie: A blues style played on the piano with a fast beat.

Chords: Where multiple notes are played at the same time at different pitches.

Chord Progression: A sequence of different musical chords in a particular pattern.

Coda: A passage of music at the end of a piece that brings it to a close.

DS (Dal Segno) al Coda: When you see this in music it means you should return and play the music from 'dal segno' (the sign) until you are told to go to the coda (the end).

Dynamics: The volume of the note produced, how loud or quiet it is.

Grace Notes (acciaccatura's): An extra note added to embellish the melody and it is played very quickly so it can be only heard for a moment.

I-P

Key Changes: Also known as modulation. When the key of the piece of music moves up or down to a different key.

Major and Minor Thirds: A type of musical interval where the notes played are one third apart.

Middle 8: Part of a piece, towards the middle of it, that tends to have a different feel to the rest of the piece and is usually 8 bars long.

Minimalism: A simplified style with minimal embellishment, in which small changes occur often throughout a piece.

Molto: An Italian term meaning 'very'.

Molto Expressivo: An Italian term meaning 'very expressive'.

Pause (Fermata): A sign to indicate a long note or rest, which is held for longer than the bar length.

Q-Z

Quavers: British way of saying an Eighth note.

Ritardando (rit): Where music gradually slows down.

Rubato: Using rhythmic freedom to slightly speed up and then slow down a piece of music in order to make it more expressive.

Sforzando: A strong, sudden accent on the note or chord.

Staccato: A note that is shortened from it's original value, so that it becomes separated from the others around it.

Syncopation: The moving of rhythm within a piece of music to make parts of the bar other than the main beats prominent.

Tempo: The pace or speed that a section of music is played at.

Time Signature: 2 numbers at the beginning of a piece of music (or midway through if there is a change) which shows how many beats are in a bar (top number) and what note value is the same as one beat (bottom number).